W9-BPM-817

Sea Animal Quiz

What is this mysterious giant?

It's Big...

As in, it's the biggest creature that ever lived, larger than a brontosaurus and a Tyrannosaurus rex put together. Its tongue weighs as much as an elephant. Its heart is as big as a car. And some of its blood vessels are so wide that a person could swim down them. The largest one ever measured was 108 feet long and weighed almost 190 tons. If you stood one of these giants on its tail, it would be as tall as a 10-story building.

And Fast ...

It can swim at speeds of up to 48 mph, making it one of the fastest swimmers in the world.

And Hungry....

It spends its summers in the icy waters around Antarctica eating krill, tiny shrimp-like crustaceans that live there in huge swarms. A single one of these creatures can eat 40 million krill in a day.

And Loud!

Our mystery mammal is the loudest creature ever recorded. A jet plane can reach a volume of 120 decibels. A gunshot might hit 140 decibels. But this monster's call clocks in at 180 decibels and can be heard for thousands of miles underwater.

WHAT IS IT?

The Cutting Edge

Some rascally pirate has removed all the consonants from the words below. Your job, matey, is to put them back where they belong. If you get stumped on a word, use the corresponding clue on the back of this sheet. *But beware!* For every clue you use, you must fill in a body part on the hanged man. If you fill in all the parts before you complete all the words...you lose!

1. _ A _
2. _ A _ O _
3. _ _ O _ _
4. _ A Y O _ E _
5. _ A _ _ _ E _
6. _ A _ _ E _ E
7. _ _ I _ E _ _ O
8. _ A _ _ _ _ I _ E

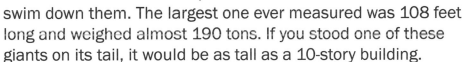

B	C	D	F	H	J	K	L	M	N	R	S	T	W	Z
C				H		K			N	R	S	T	W	
C				H						R	S	T		
												T		
												T		
												T		
												T		
												T		

Hints: Cross off each letter as you use it. All but one of these things can cut, and the one that can't has a cutting word at the end.

Answers

· · · · · · · · · ·

Sea Animal Quiz

IT'S A BLUE WHALE!

This marvelous creature is also one of the most mysterious. Scientists are just beginning to understand some of its habits, but there's much they still don't know, such as where it breeds, or where it migrates. Sadly, we may never find out because the blue whale has been hunted almost to extinction. Almost half a million were killed in the 19th century for their blubber. Scientists guess that there might be as few as 2,000 left. Because they are so rare, today there is a worldwide ban on hunting the blue whale.

The Cutting Edge

Clues

1. Put this 3-letter word before dust or mill to make a compound word.

2. The Z in the middle adds a cutting edge.

3. King Arthur's Excalibur is one of these.

4. This B word ends with a tool for catching butterflies or fish.

5. Another word for tomahawk.

6. Rearrange TEACH ME to find a bush whacker.

7. Small dagger or heel style.

8. Try the two K's side-by-side here.

Answers are upside down in the bottom left corner. Cover them with your hand if you don't want to peek.

8. JACKKNIFE
7. STILETTO
6. MACHETE
5. HATCHET

4. BAYONET
3. SWORD
2. RAZOR
1. SAW

The Cutting Edge: Answers

Uncle John's
FOR KIDS ONLY!

Riddle Me Timbers!

1. How much does it cost a girl pirate to get her ears pierced?

2. What's the first thing a pirate does when he falls overboard?

3. What do you get when you cross a pirate with a zucchini?

4. What color is bad luck for pirates?

5. What do you call a lady pirate with a sword?

6. Where is the men's room on a pirate ship?

Water World

- 71% of Earth's surface is water.

- 80% of all life lives in the ocean.

- If you were to stand at the deepest spot in the ocean, the water pressure would feel as if you were trying to lift up fifty Boeing 747s.

- If you removed the salt in the ocean, you could cover all the land on Earth in a layer of salt five feet deep.

- There's as much ice in Antarctica as there is water in the Atlantic Ocean.

- What's the tallest mountain on Earth? It's mostly underwater. Mauna Kea in Hawaii rises 33,465 feet from the ocean floor, beating Mt. Everest by more than 3,000 feet.

Secret-Sea

Figure out the riddles by writing down the first letter of each picture. Then match your answer with the correct joke.

1.

2.

3.

4.

5.

6.

A. What is a pirate's favorite kind of fish?

B. What do Kraken eat for dinner?

C. How many tickles does it take to make an octopus laugh?

D. What do you get if you cross a cat with a parrot?

E. What is a pirate's favorite state?

F. What do you call a lazy crayfish?

Answers

Riddle Me Timbers

1. The same as a male pirate: a buck an ear (a buccaneer)

2. gets wet

3. a squashbuckler

4. maroon

5. sir

6. on the poop deck

Secret Sea

A. 5. Goldfish

B. 3. Fish and Ships

C. 1. Tentacles

D. 6. Carrot

E. 4. Arrrkansas

F. 2. Slobster

Uncle John's FOR KIDS ONLY!

Captain Fromage De Mer and the Sea Flea Maze

The sea flea wants to find his way from the Captain's smelly head to his smelly boots, where his sea flea mates are. Want to join him? Well hold your nose and start hoppin'!

Answers

· · · · · · · · · · ·

Captain Fromage De Mer and the Sea Flea Maze

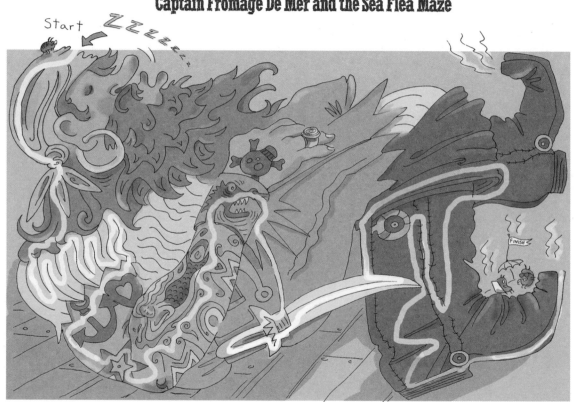

Yo Ho Ho!

Avast, ye landlubbers! If ye wanna be a pirate, get your sea legs by taking this quiz afore ye set sail.

1. When a pirate is "tipping the blackspot," he is
   a. making a death threat.
   b. swabbing a dirty deck.
   c. removing his eye patch.

2. What is a "poop deck"?
   a. the place where sea gulls like to poop on a ship
   b. the deck above the captain's quarters at the stern (rear) of the ship
   c. where pirates go to the bathroom, also known as the "head"

3. When a pirate "takes a caulk," he is
   a. taking a nap on deck.
   b. brushing his teeth.
   c. going to the bathroom.

4. What are "long clothes"?
   a. rough weather gear pirates wore when sailing through hurricanes
   b. dresses female pirates wear
   c. baggy pants and loose jackets that only landlubbers wear

5. What is a Yellow Jack?
   a. pirate slang for a yellow jacket
   b. the name of a legendary sea monster known to have sunken many a ship to "Davy Jones' locker"
   c. A warning flag. When a Yellow Jack is flown, it means there's a contagious illness (like the plague) on board.

Ship Shape

Number these 10 pictures to show in what order this model was put together.

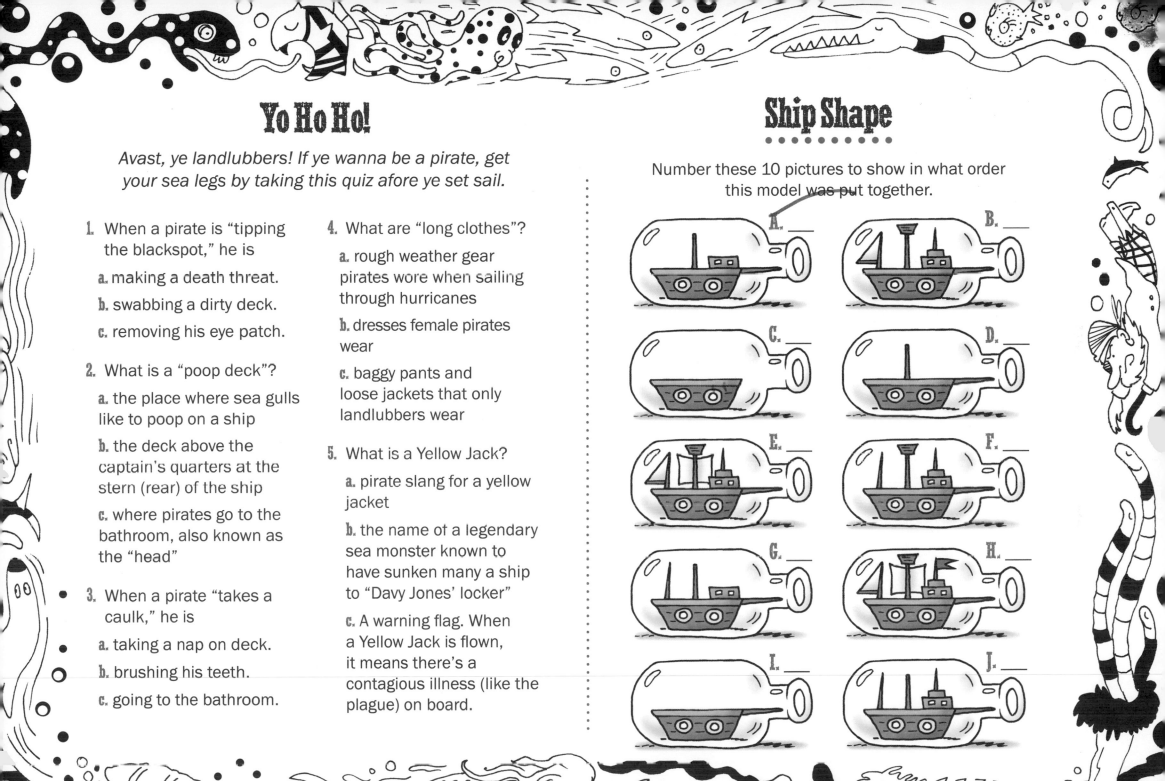

Answers

· · · · · · · · · · ·

Yo Ho Ho

1. a) When a pirate delivers a death threat, he slips his victim a piece of paper with a black smudge on one side.

2. b) A poop deck is the highest deck on a sailing ship.

3. a) A "caulk" of black tar and rope was stuffed between the planks on a ship's deck to keep water from leaking in. When pirates slept on deck, they'd often wake up with black lines across their faces from the caulk.

4. c) Pirates couldn't risk wearing anything loose fitting that might get in their way while climbing the masts to trim the sails in foul weather.

5. c) Merchant ships often flew a Yellow Jack to keep pirate ships from attacking them.

Ship Shape

A. 4; B. 8; C. 1; D. 3; E. 9;
F. 7; G. 5; H. 10; I. 2; J. 6

S. O. S.

Seven things you can do to Save Our Seas.

The ocean makes most of the oxygen we breathe. It cleans the water we drink. It gives us food and even medicine. These seven simple steps can help protect our ocean and the wildlife that lives in and near the sea.

1. Keep the ocean clean. Take your trash home with you, even if there's a trashcan on the beach.

2. Protect the sand dunes. Don't walk or play on them. They help prevent erosion.

3. Protect wildlife. Avoid nesting areas, and don't bother or chase sea birds or animals.

4. Fish smart. Keep what you can eat and release the rest. Take all fishing lines and nets home, even the broken ones. Birds and fish can get tangled in them and die.

5. Don't let go of that balloon! Sea turtles can mistake balloons (and plastic bags) for their favorite food, jellyfish, which can be a fatal mistake.

6. Reduce your greenhouse gas footprint. When you walk, ride your bike, turn off the lights, and recycle, you produce fewer greenhouse gasses. That helps reduce global warming which can help keep the oceans at temperatures that support wildlife.

7. Learn everything you can about the ocean. Share what you've learned with your friends. They might be inspired to help protect the ocean, too.

And...on June 8th, celebrate World Ocean Day.

Sea-ing Squares

Some people consider the octopus to be one of the smartest animals on the planet but this one looks stumped. Can you help him figure out how many any-size squares are shown here?

Answers

· · · · · · · · · · · ·

Sea-ing Squares

Answer: 12

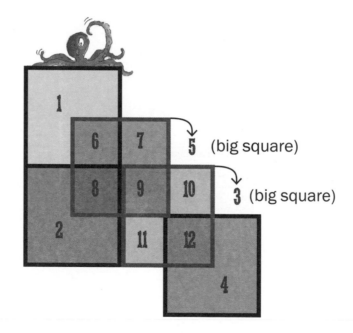

5 (big square)

3 (big square)

Yo Ho Ho!

Avast, me hearties! I vow by me eyepatch, me salty parrot, and me stout peg leg that ye need to be circlin' these terms, or we'll have ye walkin' the plank! Oh yeah, and shiver me timbers, too!

ANNE BONNY

BLACKBEARD

CAPTAIN BLOOD

CUTLASS

DAVY JONES

EARRINGS

EYE PATCH

JACK SPARROW

JEAN LAFITTE

MARY READ

PARROT

PATCHY THE PIRATE

PEG LEG

PIRATE AUNTY

```
                          V
        H F M I E A C D E
        J H C G N H A A Z
          G R M N U V R C G
          D A E R Y R A M G
            B H J I A E K D
            O C O N L A W S
            N T N G G L E R        C X
            M N A E S A B P        I O
  A           M O E Y P S T A B    I O S
  N                   E Y          S
  S S H Y             E Y          S F Y
    C P A T C H Y T H E P I R A T E A X L
    C A P T A I N B L O O D F D L G H
    H R S P I R A T E A U N T Y G
    D R A E B K C A L B U M I
      W O R R A P S K C A J
      E T T I F A L N A E J
```

DAVY JONES' LOCKER

Sure, we all know the guy had a locker, but who WAS he?

For centuries, when a sailor was drowned at sea, his mates would say, "He's gone to Davy Jones' Locker," meaning he was buried at the bottom of the sea. But where did the phrase come from? The first written reference to Davy Jones was in the 1751 novel *The Adventures of Peregrine Pickle*. Jones was described as a real sea devil with saucer-like eyes, three rows of teeth, horns, a tail, and blue smoke coming out of his nose. The 2006 movie *Pirates of the Caribbean: Dead Man's Chest* presented Davy Jones as an evil mutant mix of human and octopus. But how did he get the name Davy Jones? One theory says "Davy" comes from St. David, the patron saint of sailors. "Jones" could come from Jonah, the Biblical seaman who was swallowed by a whale.

But there's another legend. According to this story, Davy Jones was a 16th century Welsh innkeeper with a nasty side business: He would get sailors drunk enough to pass out. Then he'd stick them in his ale locker (a room used to store barrels of ale) until helpers arrived with a cart. They would haul the unconscious sailors to the nearest ship that needed crewmen. Jones got a tidy fee for each "delivery." As for the sailor, he'd wake up far out to sea, with a headache...and the worst shock of his life.

Answers

· · · · · · · · · ·

Yo Ho Ho!

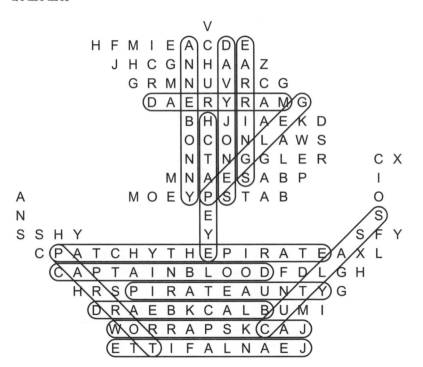

Uncle John's

FOR KIDS ONLY!

Kraken' Up

The Kraken has surfaced for a tasty ship snack. But the pictures are out of order. Can you number the squares from 1 to 9 in order of how it happened?

Hey, Let Go of My Boat!

The skies were clear, the wind crisp. Olivier de Kersauson's sleek racing boat was speeding through the deep ocean off the island of Madeira in the South Atlantic. The veteran French sailor and his crew were just beginning an around-the-world race to win the prestigious Jules Verne Trophy, when all at once they got the surprise of their lives. De Kersauson was below deck when the hull shuddered and the boat slowed down abruptly. Looking out the porthole, he saw a monstrous tentacle thicker than his leg. Rushing up on deck, he found two other tentacles wrapped around the rudder. A giant squid 24 feet long had grabbed hold of the yacht and wouldn't let go. Luckily for de Kersauson, he didn't have to fight off the monster—as soon as the boat came to a stop, the giant squid released the boat and slid beneath the waves.

"We didn't have anything to scare off this beast, so I don't know what we would have done if it hadn't let go," de Kersauson said later. "We weren't going to attack it with our penknives."

Answers

· · · · · · · · · · ·

Kraken' Up

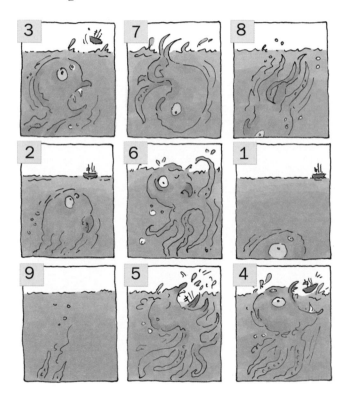

Parrot Predicament

Fill in the words below to match the pictures. Then write those words in the boxes to the right so that the letters in the pink boxes line up. There's only one way to solve the riddle. You'll know when you can read the words in the pink boxes from the top down.

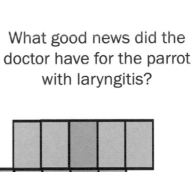

What good news did the doctor have for the parrot with laryngitis?

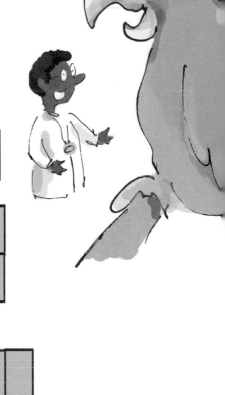

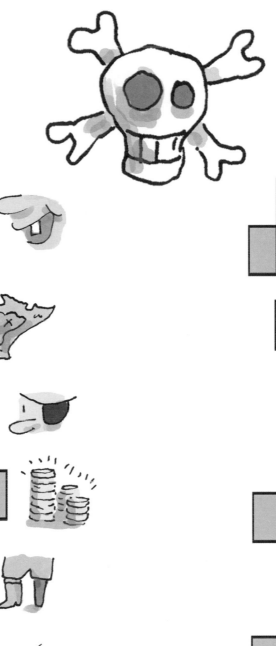

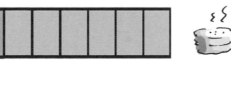

Answers

Parrot Predicament

Feather, tooth, treasure, map, ocean,
eyepatch, sails, doubloons, pirate,
pegleg, sword, biscuit

Joke answer:
It's tweetable

Pencil Race

Put your pencil point in an orange circle. Close your eyes and try to draw a line to the red winner's circle. Stop whenever you want, open your eyes, and take a look. If your pencil point isn't in the red circle, close your eyes again, and continue from where you left off. It counts as 5 seconds each time you open your eyes. Touching or crossing a blue line also adds 5 seconds (if you cross a line, back up to where you crossed it, then take your next turn from there).

100 meters (world record: 15 seconds)

200 meters (world record: 25 seconds)

Obstacle course (world record: 45 seconds)

Now it's your turn! Invent your own courses.

Get the lead out!

ZZZZZzz

Uncle John's

FOR KIDS ONLY!

Polly-Wanna-Doku

Get out your squid ink and draw pictures in the empty boxes so that they follow the rules in the example below.

 Wheel

 Bones

 Parrot

 Skull

All 4 pictures in each column

All 4 pictures in each row →

All 4 pictures in each bold box →

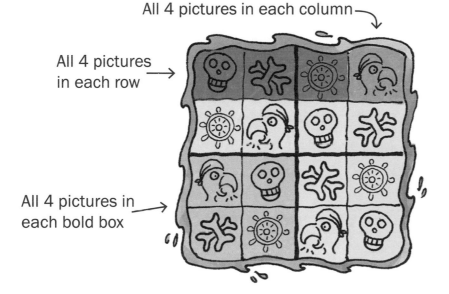

1.

2.

3.

Hardy-Har Har-r-r!

Q: Why couldn't the pirate play cards?

A: He was standing on the deck.

Answers

Polly-Wanna-Doku

1.

2.

3.

Uncle John's
FOR KIDS ONLY!

Sea Doodles

Draw Your Own Sea Doodles

Match the words with the drawings.

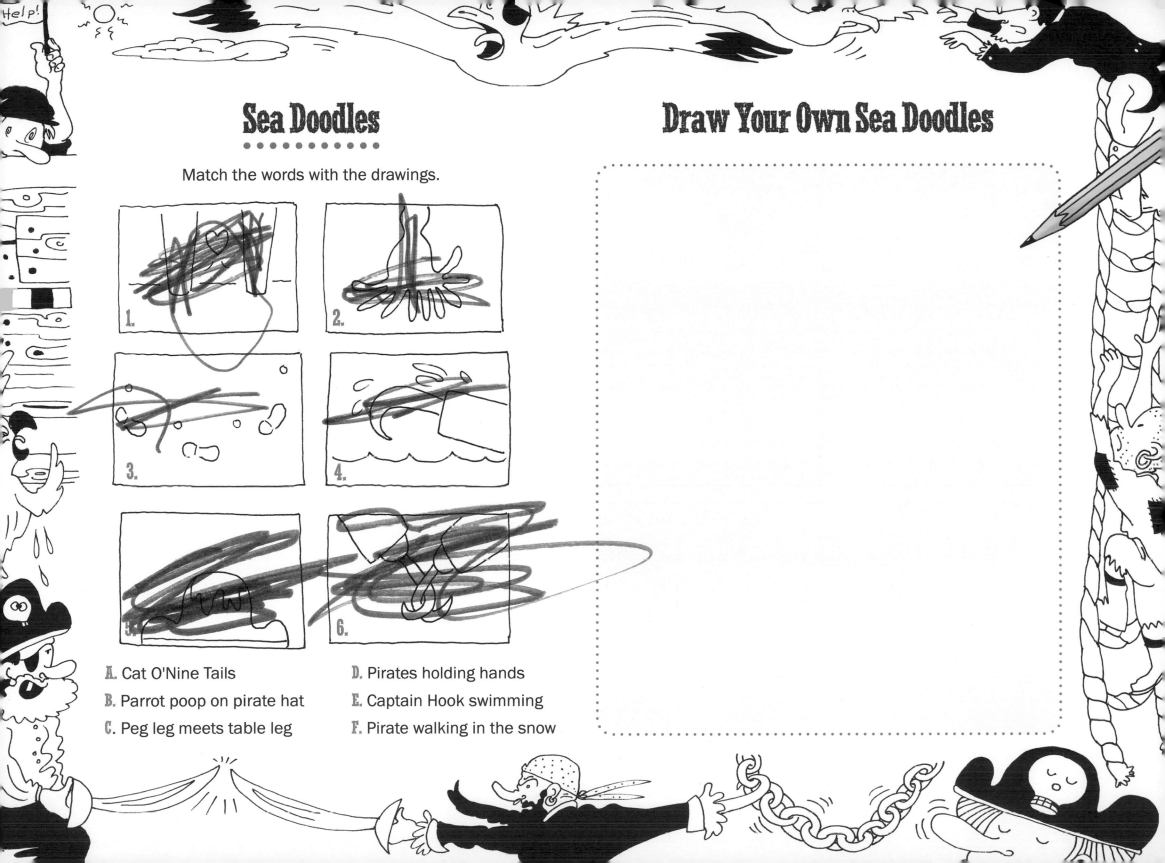

1.

2.

3.

4.

5.

6.

A. Cat O'Nine Tails

B. Parrot poop on pirate hat

C. Peg leg meets table leg

D. Pirates holding hands

E. Captain Hook swimming

F. Pirate walking in the snow

Answers
. . . .

Sea Doodles

A. 2

B. 5

C. 1

D. 6

E. 4

F. 3

Uncle John's
FOR KIDS ONLY!

Shark Facts

- Sharks have no bones. Their skeletons are made of cartilage, the same stuff that's in your ears and your nose.

- Sharks are ancient. They were patrolling the oceans more than 300 million years ago—nearly 75 million years before the dinosaurs were around.

- Scientists think sharks were the first creatures to have teeth.

- A shark can detect a single drop of blood in a million drops (25 gallons) of water.

- If it doesn't keep swimming, a shark will sink.

- Sharks can sense vibrations in water, and they can detect electrical currents. They use these skills to find their prey.

HARDY-HAR HAR-R-R!

Q: What happens when you throw a red rock into the Black Sea?

A: It sinks.

Q: What happens when you throw a green rock into the Red Sea?

A: It gets wet.

Size Them Up

We've drawn these around-the-word ships about the same size—but they're not! Try numbering them in order of how LONG you think they actually are, from shortest to longest. Then follow the lines to see if you're right.

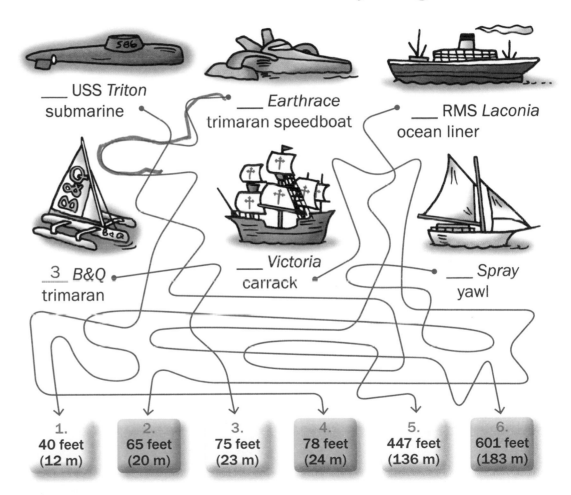

___ USS *Triton* submarine

___ *Earthrace* trimaran speedboat

___ RMS *Laconia* ocean liner

_3_ *B&Q* trimaran

___ *Victoria* carrack

___ *Spray* yawl

1. 40 feet (12 m)
2. 65 feet (20 m)
3. 75 feet (23 m)
4. 78 feet (24 m)
5. 447 feet (136 m)
6. 601 feet (183 m)

Riddle Me Factoid! Pirates charged with firing cannons during attacks dangled wax from their gold earrings to use as earplugs when needed.

Answers

· · · · · · · · · · ·

Size Them Up

1. *Spray* was 40 feet long.
2. *Victoria* was about 65 feet long.
3. *B&Q* is 75 feet long.
4. *Earthrace* is 78 feet long.
5. USS *Triton* is 447 feet long.
6. RMS *Laconia* was 601 feet long.

Uncle John's

FOR KIDS ONLY!

Here Be Treasure!

Tales of pirate gold, lost and found...

Ever dream of finding buried pirate booty? Travel to the Costa Rican island of Cocos and you may get a two-for-one. In 1818, somewhere in the island's tree-covered hills, Benito "Bloody Sword" Bonito buried a load of Spanish gold worth $300 million. In 1820 another pirate, William Thompson, hijacked the legendary Treasure of Lima (the wealth of more than 50 churches in the Peruvian capital), and stashed it on Cocos. Since then, hundreds of treasure hunters have scoured the island—including President Franklin Roosevelt—but no one has ever found either hoard.

. . . .

HARDY-HAR HAR-R-R!

Q: Why are fish smarter than mice?

A: Because they live in schools.

Q: What do you call a fish with no eye?

A: FSH!

Ship's Wheel of Fortune

. . . .

What has 12 legs, 12 arms and 12 eyes?

Arr, mateys, here's how to find the answer:
Start at the arrow. Write that letter in the first space below. Continue around the wheel in the direction shown, writing down EVERY OTHER letter (you'll have to go around the wheel twice).

Answer: __ __ __ __ __

__ __ __ __ __ __

Answers

· · · · · · · · · · ·

Ship's Wheel of Fortune

ONE DOZEN PIRATES

Draw Rollo & Bob

Follow the steps in order. Sketch in pencil first. When you're happy with your sketch, trace over your lines in ink. Let the ink dry, then erase the pencil lines.

1. 2. 3. 4.

5. 6.

1. 2. 3. 4.

Draw a Rollo & Bob Comic Strip

Add Rollo and Bob to these four comic-strip panels. Are they standing, walking, sitting? Are they close up or far away? What are they doing with their arms?

Hey, Rollo. Why do you have that eye patch?

Because I can't afford an iPad.

Bob, why'd you toss that hot dog?

It was a salty dog.

Come up with your own jokes for these two panels:

Uncle John's

FoR
KIDS
ONLY!

Snorkel Masters

Did you know that elephants can snorkel? They can walk along the bottom of a river with just the tip of their trunks sticking out for air. They have even been seen snorkeling far out at sea. Some scientists think elephants may have evolved from water creatures because of their snorkeling ability.

Did you know?

- Elephants' eyes are only slightly larger than humans'.

- The average elephant weighs less than a blue whale's tongue.

- There are 40,000 muscles in an elephant's trunk.

- Elephants can hear the footsteps of a mouse.

- Elephants cry when a loved one dies.

Riddle Me Factoid!

In 1553, China's kung-fu-fighting Shaolin monks were called on to repel Japanese pirates raiding their coastline. They succeeded.

Down the Drain

There's treasure beneath the lake. To find it, follow the drain from START to END.

start

End!

Answers

· · · · · · · · · · ·

Down the Drain

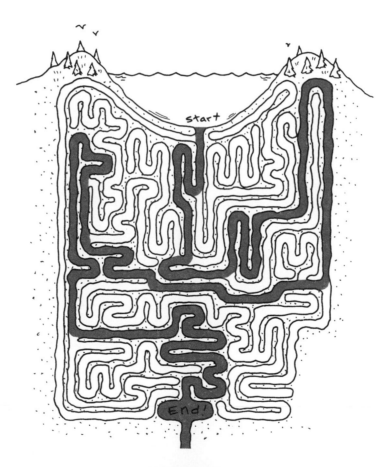

Ocean Oddballs

Gathered together for the first time ever are some of the oddest piratical oddballs on the high seas. Your job, swabby, is to match names to pictures.

1. Davey Jones
2. Captain Clipper
3. Cat O'Nine Tails
4. Sea Wolf
5. Bucaneer

6. Salty Dog
7. Jolly Roger
8. Jack O'Cups
9. Cabin boy
10. Cackle fruit

Want To Be a Pirate?

Combine a name from column 1, column 2, and column 3 in any order to create your pirate name. Then draw what you would look like on the back of the placemat.

1	2	3
Dirty	Jack	Barnacle
Peg Leg	Sealegs	Fishbreath
Jolly	Mc	Bilgewater
Smelly	Scurvy	Shrimpnose
Captain	Queenie	O'Greedy

A.

B.

C.

D.

E.

F.

G.

H.

I.

J.

Answers

Ocean Oddballs:

1. F

2. I

3. D

4. A

5. E

6. G

7. H

8. B

9. C

10. J

Pumpkin Island

Avast, ye landlubbers! It's time to get off yer duffs and get to work. Your job? Read the description below. Then draw Pumpkin Island in all its glorious and gory details.

Pumpkin Island is home to the notorious Pumpkin Pirates. Huge pumpkins grow here. The pirates hollow them out and turn them into boats. Then they sail to sea to prey and pillage. (Pumpkin Island appears in *True History* written by Lucian of Samosta around AD 200.)

Uncle John's

FOR KIDS ONLY!

Tying the Knot

Whether you're a sailor, surgeon, fisherman, or climber, there will come a time when you'll need to know your knots. The grid shape is in honor of a pattern familiar to boy scouts everywhere—the diamond knot.

ANCHOR BEND

ARBOR

AXLE HITCH

BOWLINE

BUTTERFLY

CATS PAW

DIAMOND

EYE SPLICE

FIADOR

FIGURE OF EIGHT

FLEMISH

GORDIAN

GRANNY

GRIEF

HANDCUFF

LARKS HEAD

NOOSE

POWER CINCH

SAVOY

SHEET BEND

SLIP KNOT

SPLICE

TARBUCK

UNI

YOSEMITE BOWLINE

ZEPPELIN BEND

```
                    G
                  R P Y
                A R B O R
              N X O U S W Z
            N A L D T E S E B
          Y D I E A T M L P R E
        S I N D H I E I I P L C K
      W H U O R I F R T P E D I I B
    C J E U M O T I F E K L A L C N D
  D V A E N A G C G L B N I E P G E C G
D G V K T O I L H U Y O O N H S L E P H Z
  H V Y B S D L J R V W T B S E Q G S D
    A G E P P P W E J L A E K Y Q I N
      N N F S A V O Y I R N R E M E
        D N E S W F B N B D A E B
          C N I D E E E U R L R
            U M R I O S C F O
              F R G A O K H
                F H I O C
                  T J N
                    A
```

Dolphin Facts

- Dolphins are born with mustaches. (So are whales.)

- A dolphin can hold its breath for up to eight minutes and dive as deep as 1,000 feet.

- Dolphins sleep with one eye shut—half of their brain rests; the other half (and the other eye) stays awake.

Answers

· · · · · · · · · ·

Tying the Knot

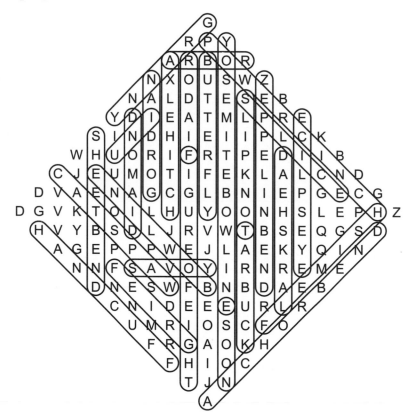

Uncle John's
FOR KIDS ONLY!

Jail, to a Jailbird

Some rascally pirate has removed all the consonants from the words below. Your job, matey, is to put them back into the words where they belong. If you get stumped on a word, use the corresponding clue on the back of this sheet. *But beware!* For every clue you use, you must fill in a body part on the hanged man. If you fill in all the parts before you complete all the words...you lose! If not...arrr! You win!

1. _ _ I _
2. _ _ I _ _
3. _ O I _ _
4. _ O _ E Y
5. _ O O _ E _
6. _ O _ _ U _
7. _ _ A _ _ E _
8. _ O O _ E _ O _

C G H J K L M N P R S T W
C   K L M N P R S T
C   K L   R S
         L

Surfin' Snails

They ride the surf to catch their dinner!

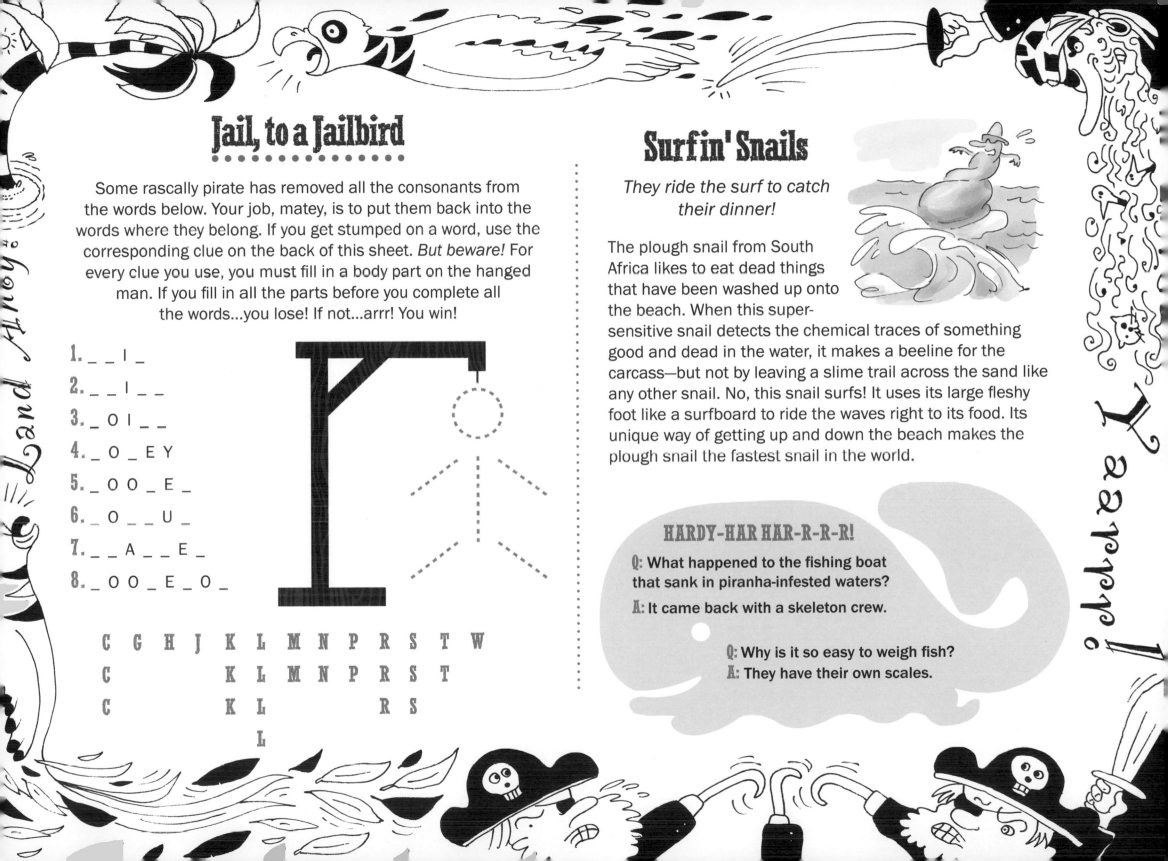

The plough snail from South Africa likes to eat dead things that have been washed up onto the beach. When this super-sensitive snail detects the chemical traces of something good and dead in the water, it makes a beeline for the carcass—but not by leaving a slime trail across the sand like any other snail. No, this snail surfs! It uses its large fleshy foot like a surfboard to ride the waves right to its food. Its unique way of getting up and down the beach makes the plough snail the fastest snail in the world.

HARDY-HAR HAR-R-R-R!

Q: What happened to the fishing boat that sank in piranha-infested waters?

A: It came back with a skeleton crew.

Q: Why is it so easy to weigh fish?

A: They have their own scales.

Answers

· · · · · · · · · ·

Jail, to a Jailbird

Clues

1. Best done with a spoon.

2. "C" plus part of a chain.

3. The J goes first.

4. Rhymes with hokey.

5. Cold drink carrier.

6. Four of the letters in "pocket" are here.

7. LAM fits into this word.

8. Starts with H.

Answers are upside down in the bottom left corner. Cover them with your hand if you don't want to peek.

Answers

1. STIR
2. CLINK
3. JOINT
4. POKEY
5. COOLER
6. LOCKUP
7. SLAMMER
8. HOOSEGOW

Get The Governor

Pirates have landed! They're off to grab the governor and all the booty in his mansion. Can you beat them from the ship and warn him?

Start

Finish

Answers

· · · · · · · · · · ·

Get the Governor

Bartholomew Goes Bad

Bartholomew "Black Bart" Roberts came to piracy late (he was 37), but he was the most successful pirate of all time. Born in Wales, he roamed the seas from Brazil to Africa to Newfoundland, capturing and looting more than 400 ships during his career. He designed his own pirate flag, which had a giant figure of himself, cutlass in hand, standing on two skulls. Roberts' life of crime came to an end when he was killed by a hail of gunfire in a battle off the coast of West Africa in 1722.

It's your turn! Design your personal pirate flag.

Mom: Did you give the goldfish fresh water today?

Kid: No, they haven't finished the water I gave them yesterday.

Gnarly Teeth the Quiz!

Only one answer to each description is a real animal. The others are phonies. Can you guess the real one?

1. This creature's nose is lined with long, pointed teeth. When it swims into a school of fish, it whips its snout around like a samurai sword, slashing fish left and right. If something good to eat is buried in the sand, it uses its nose like a rake to get at it.

   a. Clam-rake shark   c. Spear shark

   b. Sawshark   d. Samurai shark

2. It swims with its mouth slightly open, so it can breathe. On the hunt, it locks onto its target like a streamlined torpedo. This predator has 3,000 teeth in seven rows in its mouth. When a tooth breaks off, the one behind it moves forward and takes its place.

   a. Torpedo shark   c. Great white shark

   b. Mega-toothed shark   d. Sandpaper shark

3. This animal looks like it has a jousting lance attached to its head. The lance is actually a long, spiraled tooth. The animal is often seen floating on its back, its tusk pointing up at the sky. In medieval times, its tusks were sold as unicorn horns.

   a. Unicorn whale   c. Spiraled-tusked whale

   b. King Arthur's whale   d. Narwhal

Answers

· · · · · · · · · ·

Gnarly Teeth-The Quiz

1. b) The sawshark is actually a ray. Like other sharks and rays, it has special receptors on its snout that help it detect tiny electrical impulses of live prey. It's not a danger to humans—unless you happen to get in the way of its nasty sharp nose.

2. c) The great white shark's teeth are made for grabbing and tearing. But these teeth are more sensitive than your fingertips. That's why great white sharks "mouth" their prey first, to see if it's tasty enough to eat. But the taste-test can be bad news for most animals: Even if the great white decides not to take a second bite, the "mouthing" is often fatal.

3. d) The narwhal's mysterious tusk (its left front tooth, actually) is the only spiraled tusk in nature. And, unlike most teeth, it's soft on the outside and hard on the inside. It is so sensitive that the narwhal may be able to detect changes in weather—which is important when you live in the icy waters of the Arctic Ocean.

Water World

- 97% of the Earth's water is in the ocean. Less than 1% is fresh water.

- 99% percent of the living space on the Earth is under water. (Less than 10% of that space has been explored.)

- There's enough gold in the ocean to give a nine-pound chunk to every person in the world.

- The weight of the garbage dumped into the ocean every year is more than three times the weight of the fish caught in the same year.

- If you removed the salt in the ocean, you could cover all the land on Earth in a layer of salt five feet deep.

- If you were to stand at the deepest spot in the ocean, the water pressure would feel as if you were trying to lift up *fifty* Boeing 747s.

Pigeon Towed

At right is a message carried by a heroic pigeon named Cher Ami during World War I. Despite being shot in the chest and leg, he completed his flight, saving the lives of 200 soldiers. Which route should he follow to bring it to headquarters?

We are along the road parallel to 276.4. Our own artillery is dropping a barrage directly on us. For heaven's sake, stop it.

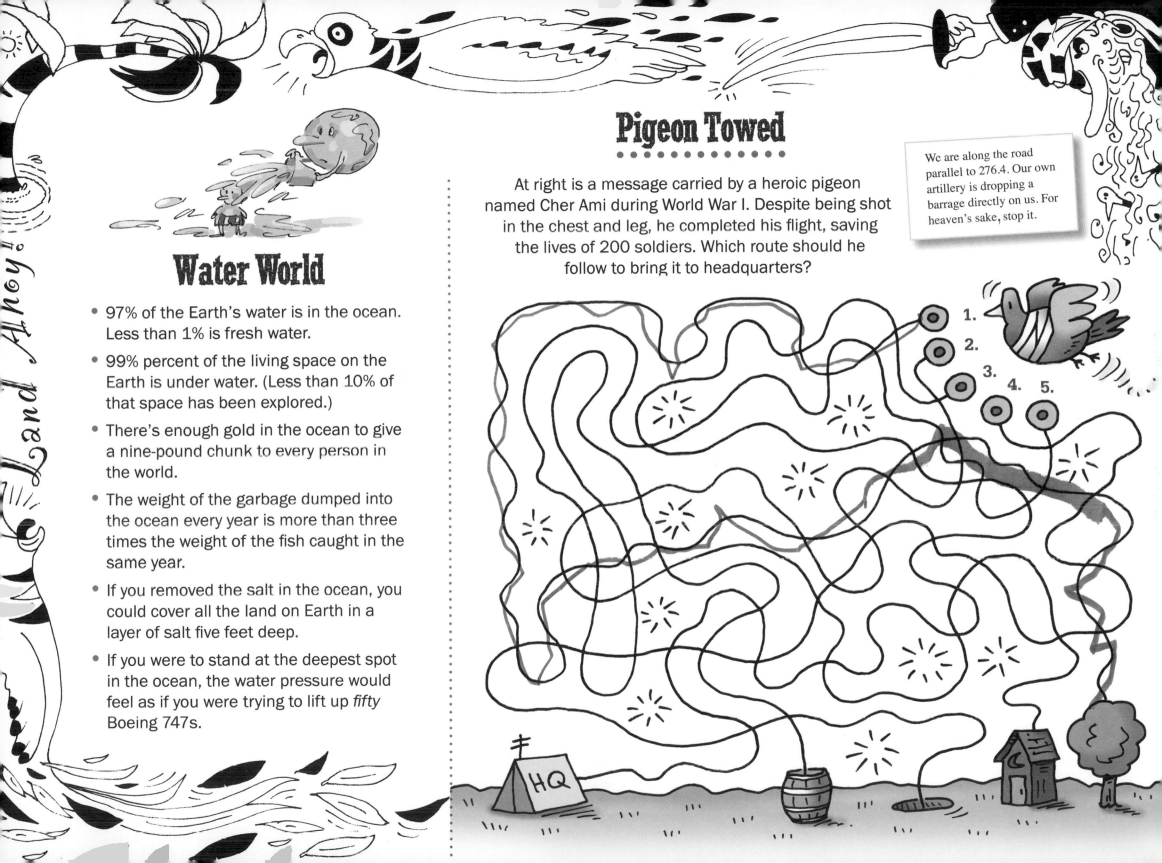

Answers

· · · · · · · · · · ·

Pigeon Towed

3 leads to the headquarters (HQ) tent.

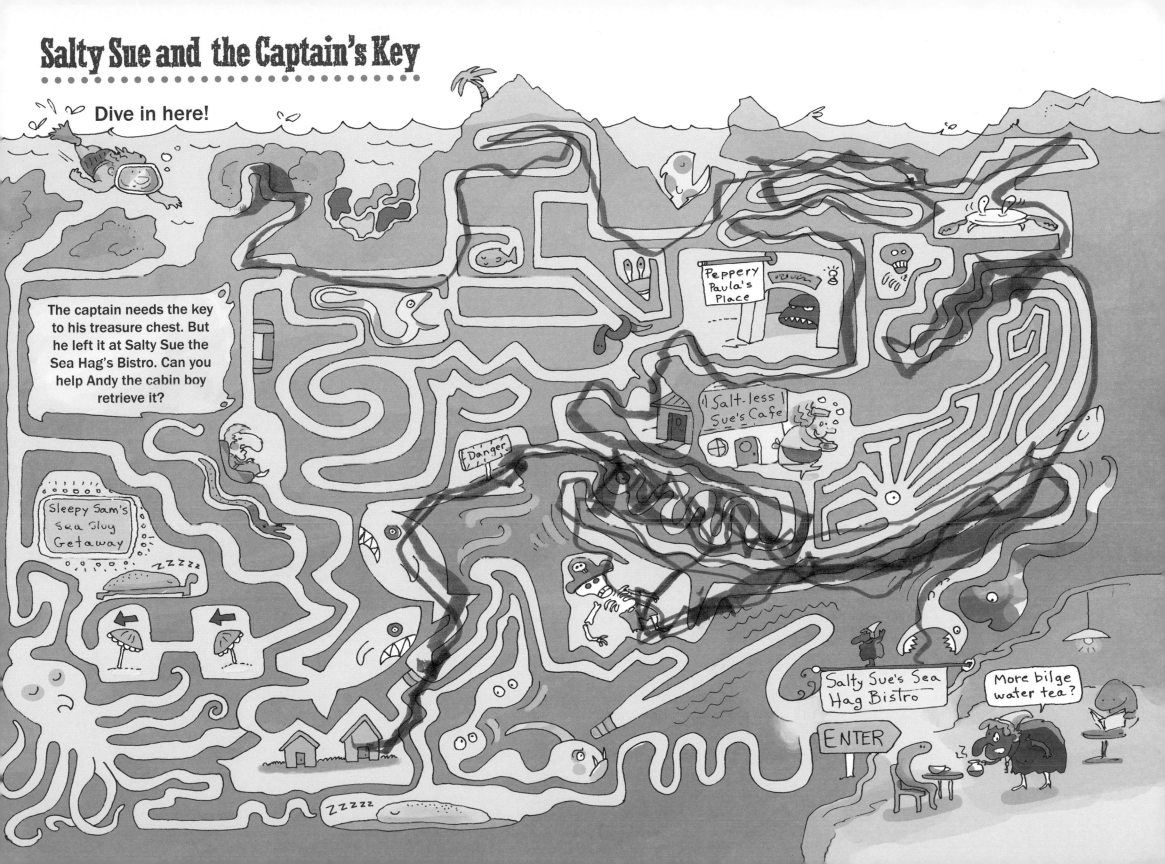

Answers

Salty Sue and the Captain's Key

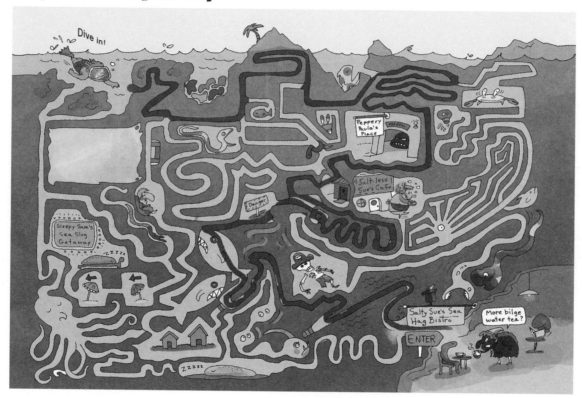

E-w-w-w!

In December 2006, an alarm went off in the aquarium at the Weymouth Sea Life Center in England. Marine biologist Sarah Leaney raced to the tank to see what was wrong, but found nothing out of order. As she looked at the alarm sensor, a sea turtle floating by ripped off a couple of farts. *Br-r-r-ing!* The alarm went off again. Leaney quickly realized what had happened: The staff had fed the turtle a holiday treat of Brussels sprouts. It seemed the vegetable has the same effect on turtles as it does on people. When they eat too much of it—it produces a mighty, stinky wind!

School Daze

. . . .

Go figure!

There are 100 kids in Mrs. Gooch's second-grade class. (It's a big class—the result of friendly neighborhood budget cuts.) Of these, 85 children are dropped off at school each day by their parents, 70 carry stuffed animals, 75 like to eat cheese sandwiches at lunchtime, and 80 hate apple juice. What's the least possible number of kids who could embody all four characteristics (meaning, they are dropped off by their parents, carry stuffed animals, like cheese sandwiches, and hate apple juice)?

Shark Jokes

. . . .

A matchup for those of you who like a little bite in your humor.

1. ___ How can you tell a boy shark from a girl shark?

2. ___ What happened to the shark who swallowed a bunch of keys?

3. ___ What does a shark eat with peanut butter?

4. ___ What happens when you cross a great white shark with a cow?

5. ___ Why do sharks swim only in saltwater?

6. ___ Why don't sharks eat clowns?

7. ___ What do you get when you cross a big fish with an electric wire?

8. ___ Where do fish go when they want to borrow money?

9. ___ What do you get from a bad-tempered shark?

A. They taste funny.

B. Jellyfish.

C. I don't know—but whatever you do, don't milk it.

D. He got lockjaw.

E. Because pepper water would make them sneeze.

F. A loan shark.

G. As far away as possible!

H. You give it a fish. If he eats it, it's a boy...if she eats it, it's a girl.

I. An electric shark.

Answers

School Daze

The answer is 10. Of the 100 kids, 15 of them are not dropped off by their parents, 30 don't carry stuffed animals, 25 don't like cheese sandwiches for lunch, and 20 love apple juice. That makes 90 kids; they could all be different children. That means that the least number who can embody all four characteristics is the remaining 10.

Shark Jokes

1: H; 2: D; 3: B; 4: C; 5: E; 6: A; 7: I; 8: F; 9: G

Nine Amazing Fish Facts

These may sound fishy, but Uncle John swears they are absolutely true.

1. A lobster's teeth are in its stomach.

2. A shrimp's heart is in its head.

3. A horseshoe crab has 10 eyes. They're placed all over its body—even on its tail.

4. You can guess a fish's age by its scales. You can count the growth rings, just like you'd count the rings on a tree.

5. Fish can get seasick. Keep a fish in a pail of water on a rolling ship, and sooner or later that fish will barf.

6. Fish get dandruff. It's caused by flaking skin (as it is in humans), and there's nothing they can do about it.

7. Some fish can breathe air. Small fish like betas and gouramis have an organ called a labyrinth that lets them breathe fresh air. It allows them to survive in water with low oxygen levels.

8. Fish can talk to each other. Some rasp their teeth or make noises in their throats; other fish use their swim bladders like a horn.

9. Fish can change sex. Boy? Girl? Many fish start out as one sex and turn into the other one later on. Some deepwater fish are both sexes all the time. That means they never need to look for a mate to have babies.

Triangular Reasoning

As it is now, if you add up the four numbers on each side of the large triangle below, you'll get three different sums: 18, 16, and 22. But what you want is for each side to equal the same amount. You can accomplish that by swapping two pairs of numbers. What are the swaps, and what number do all the sides add up to?

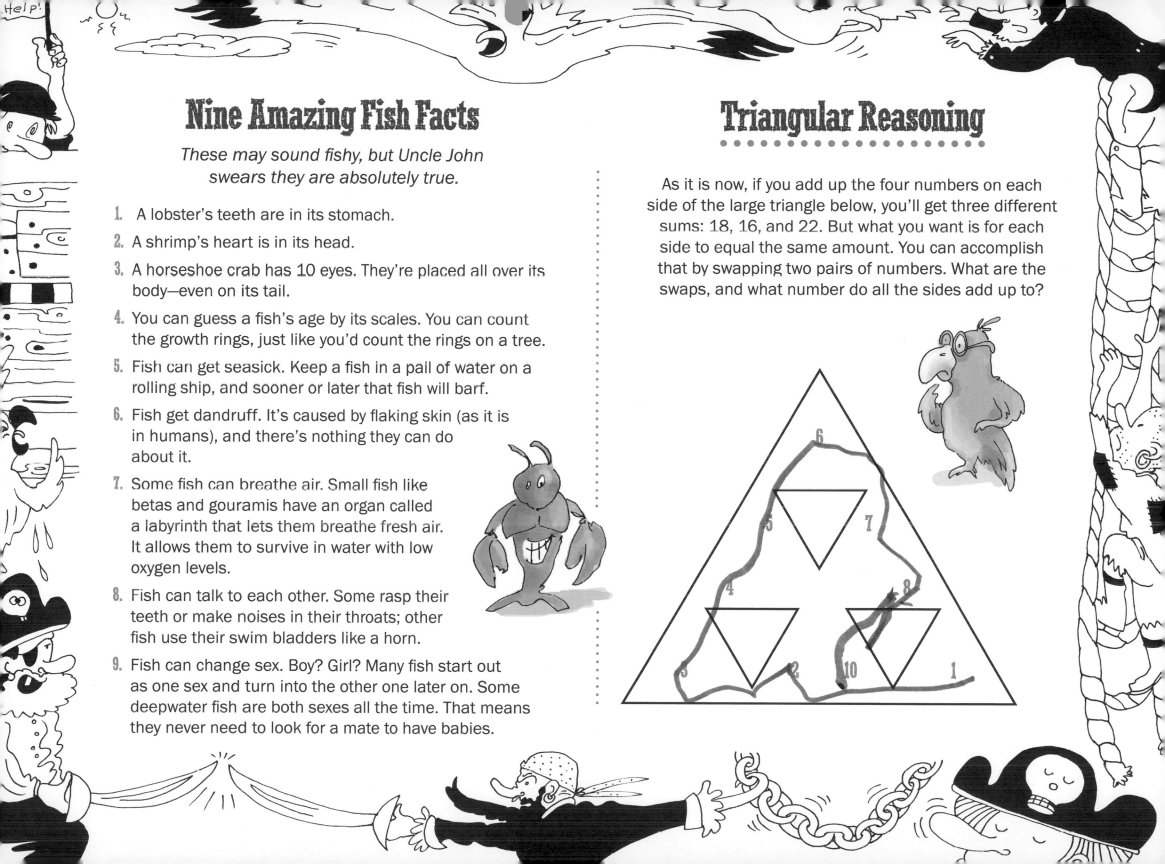

Answers

Triangular Reasoning

First swap the 5 and 7 in the second row. Then swap the 7 with the 3 in the bottom left corner. Each side will now add up to 20.

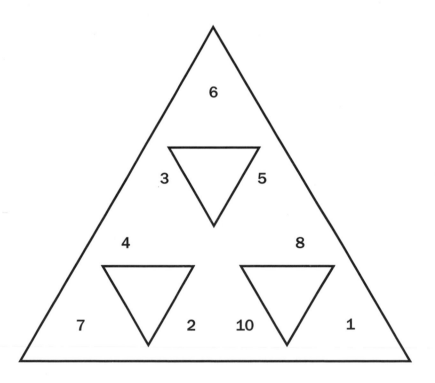

Madame Ching

One of the greatest pirates of all time was...a woman!

Madame Ching pirated the waters off the coast of China in the early years of the 19th century. At the height of her power, she commanded a fleet of 1,800 ships and 70,000 men. But she didn't get to the top by being nice. If one of her pirates broke her rules, she had his head lopped off.

Although Madame Ching terrorized the Chinese navy for years, she was able to do what few pirates ever accomplished: die of old age. In exchange for giving up piracy, the Chinese Navy granted her a pardon in 1810. Madame Ching was even allowed to keep all of her stolen treasure. She used it to open up a gambling house, which she ran for the rest of her life.

HARDY-HAR HAR-R-R!

Q: What do you get when you graduate from scuba diving school?

A: A deep-loma.

Q: Where do ghosts swim in North America?

A: In Lake Erie.

The Adventures of Madame Ching

Draw what you imagine!

Uncle John's
FOR KIDS ONLY!

Ice-udoku

Draw pictures in the ice cubes so that they follow the rules in the example.

- meteorite
- glove
- penguin
- snow

All 4 pictures in each column

All 4 pictures in each row

All 4 pictures in each group bordered by bold lines

1.

2.

3.

Answers

Ice-udoku

1.

2.  3.

Uncle John's
FOR KIDS ONLY!

The Case of the Kidnapped Kid

When Uncle John heard this tale, he immediately called in his favorite detective—Inspector Commodius Loo—to solve the crime. See if you can figure it out.

Winslow, one of Miss Shapen's students, had been kidnapped. His dad had paid the $20,000 ransom, but things had not gone as planned. Winslow was still missing, and his brother Waldo—who had delivered a gym bag full of cash to the ransom drop—had a bump on his head.

"I went to the deserted parking garage just like they said," Waldo told Inspector Loo. "But somebody conked me on the back of the head. I fell and dropped the gym bag. My attacker swooped in, grabbed it, and ran off. I never saw his face, only his back. He was tall and redheaded, wearing jeans. He had on this hoodie to help hide his face. I think it had a college logo on front."

"Anyone else around?" Loo asked.

Waldo shrugged. "Some homeless guy pushing a shopping cart. Oh, another dude drove up in a Mercedes. He wanted to call the cops, but I begged him not to. The kidnappers said no police."

"Now they want another $20,000," Miss Shapen wailed. "What should we do? Should we track down the homeless man and the Mercedes driver?"

"No need," Loo said. "I know what happened."

How did Inspector Loo crack the case, and what had he figured out?

Smells Bad!
• • • • • • • • • •

Seven animals below have a great sense of smell. By comparison, three of them don't smell as well. Each hint will eliminate one or two good smellers (check them off as you go), leaving the three bad smellers.

Eliminate any animal whose name...

...has fewer than 4 letters
...has more than 2 syllables
...has fewer than 2 vowels
...ends in E
...has fewer than 2 syllables

__ Chicken
__ Mole

__ Bear
__ Ant
__ Human
__ Shark

__ Pig
__ Dolphin
__ Snake
__ Elephant

Riddle Me Factoid! Sea pirates plagued ancient Egypt. In 1186 B.C., Pharoah Ramses III battled them at sea and ended the terrifying raids.

Q: Best time to buy a new pirate ship?
A: When it's on sail.

Answers

The Case of the Kidnapped Kid

Waldo's story had a few holes in it. He told the inspector that he'd only seen his attacker from the back. But if that were true, he couldn't have known the hoodie had a college logo on the front. And if the attacker was wearing a hoodie to hide his face, Waldo could not have seen that he had red hair. Waldo finally confessed that he and Winslow had set the whole thing up to get money from their dad. He'd refused to buy them turbo-charged dirt bikes so they could join the extreme-motocross tour. They did make it onto season two of *World's Dumbest Rich Kids*.

Smells Bad!

The three bad smellers are the chicken, the human, and the dolphin.

Play Time

Twenty-seven fun toys for kids of all ages.

ACTION FIGURES

BALLS

BARBIE DOLL

ELECTRIC TRAIN

ERECTOR SET

ETCH-A-SKETCH

HULA HOOP

JACK-IN-THE-BOX

JACKS

JUMPROPE

KALEIDOSCOPE

LEGO BRICKS

LINCOLN LOGS

MARBLES

MATCHBOX CARS

NERF BALL

NEWTON'S CRADLE

PICKUP STICKS

PLAY-DOH

PUZZLES

RUBIK'S CUBE

SILLY PUTTY

SOLDIERS

TINKERTOYS

TOP

WHISTLE

YO-YO

HARDY-HAR HAR-R-R!

Q: If they made a movie starring the Loch Ness monster and the great white shark from *Jaws*, what would the movie be called?

A: *Loch Jaws.*

```
M Y H N Q W C H F T N G L Q S I V U R
R I T I N K E R T O Y S E I V Y N S K
B R E T H H M U Y D S V Q A X O I J F
V F S X U O A Z G E E N R O N Q A A S
J S R E O P D A S O L D I E R S R T P
D K O S B B Y Y Z I Z S L H W K T D D
P C T J R U E L A R Z C L E R C C Y D
J I C L B A C H L L U T L L V I I H W
E T E M A N C S T I P T U R A R R H L
U S R O I L L X K N S O M L F B T C I
B P E L Y L J S O I I Q O T P O C T N
J U M P R O P E H B B K N H X G E E C
J K K W O D Y W M G H U C C A E L K O
B C T N N E W T O N S C R A D L E S L
M I A W C I K O Y K J M T Q J G U A N
Y P R C T B O P X U S K C A J T B H L
L L A B F R E N S E L B R A M F M C O
V U B O K A L E I D O S C O P E G T G
J V J E W B A C T I O N F I G U R E S
```

Answers

• • • • • • • • • •

Play Time

```
M Y H N Q W C H F T N G L Q S I V U R
R I T I N K E R T O Y S E I V Y N S K
B R E T H H M U Y D S V Q A X O I J F
V F S X U O A Z G E E N R O N Q A T S P
J S R E O P D A S O L D I E R S R T P
D K O S B B Y Y Z I Z S L H W K C Y D D
P C T J R U E L A R Z C L E R C I R D
J I C L B A C H L L U T L L V I R H W
E T E M A N C S T I P T U R A R R T L
U S R O I L L X K N S O M L F B T C I
B P E L Y L J S C I Q O T P O C T N
J U M P R O P E H B B K N H X G E E K C
J K K W O D Y W M G H U C C A E L E K O
B C T N N E W T O N S C R A D L E S L
M I A W C I K O Y K J M T Q J G U A N N
Y P R C T B O P X U S K C A J T B H L
L L A B F R E N S E L B R A M F M C O
V U B O K A L E I D O S C O P E G T G
J V J E W B A C T I O N F I G U R E S
```

Uncle John's
FOR
KIDS
ONLY!

Nautical Names

Each animal has a name that matches what it's doing. For example a singing seashell would be named Carol. Can you match them up?

1. Skip
2. Rose
3. Buzz
4. Juice
5. Art
6. Ruby
7. Penny
8. Rich
9. Dolly
10. Flip
11. Forrest

DRAW YOUR OWN CHARACTERS!

Use these names or make up your own: *Blaze, Melody, Misty, Lance, Woody,* and *Duke*. Hint: There's lots of room to draw on the back of the placemat.

Answers

Nautical Names

A: 3. Buzz; B: 9. Dolly; C: 7. Penny; D: 11, Forrest;
E: 2. Rose; F: 4. Juice; G: 1. Skip; H: 10. Flip;
I: 6. Ruby; J: 5. Art; K: 8. Rich

Uncle John's
FOR KIDS ONLY!

Shipshape

Ahoy, matey! We've included a handful of seagoing vessels from movies, TV, and literature in this ship-shaped list. Happy sailing!

AFRICAN QUEEN   CAINE   MINNOW   ORCA   SEA WITCH

ARGO   CALYPSO   MISSOURI   PINTA   SEA WOLF

ARIZONA   KON-TIKI   NAUTILUS   POSEIDON   THE BEAGLE

BOUNTY   LUSITANIA   NINA   SANTA MARIA   TITANIC

```
V
C S
D I C
D G N H
O U Y A J
G V E T T N
R W O N N I M
A G Q J M U T N
N O D I E S O P Q
O S P Y L A C B V
Z

K O N T I K I H C T I W A E S E A W O L F
I R U O S S I M C R E L G A E B E H T
F C M A F R I C A N Q U E E N A R
S A N T A M A R I A T N I P O
A I N A T I S U L J A C M
N A U T I L U S C X W
```

Globsters

What's shapeless, looks like goop, and stinks?

A globster is a very weird, completely baffling object that might be found on any beach. Think of a big pile of jelly-like, fatty flesh. There might be a huge tentacle or a weird-looking flipper sticking out of the goop. Sometimes it has hair, but it never has bones, scales, or cartilage. And the worst part: It stinks...a lot. Most globsters are eventually identified as the fatty remains of dead whales or giant squids. Some of the hardest to identify have turned out to be dead basking sharks, one of the largest (and strangest) fish in the ocean. But some globsters remain unidentified—a gooey, gross reminder that there are still unsolved mysteries in the deep.

HARDY-HAR HAR-R-R!

Q: What sea animal can be adjusted to play music?

A: The tune-a fish!

Q: What sits at the bottom of the sea and shivers?

A: A nervous wreck.

Answers

· · · · · · · · · · ·

Shipshape

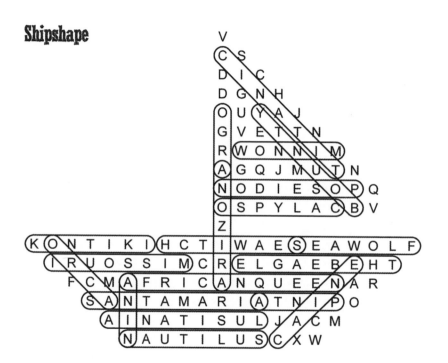

Uncle John's

FOR KIDS ONLY!

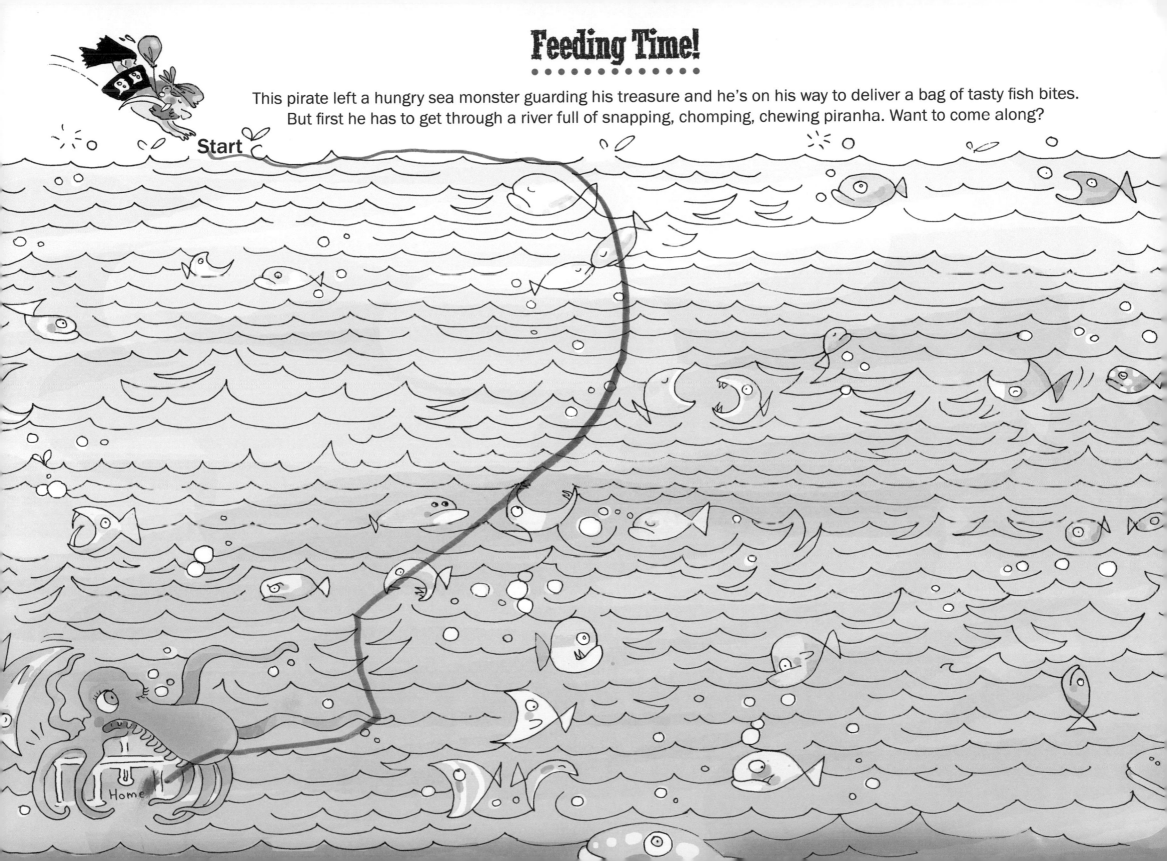

Feeding Time!

This pirate left a hungry sea monster guarding his treasure and he's on his way to deliver a bag of tasty fish bites. But first he has to get through a river full of snapping, chomping, chewing piranha. Want to come along?

Start

Home

Answers

· · · · · · · · · ·

Feeding Time!

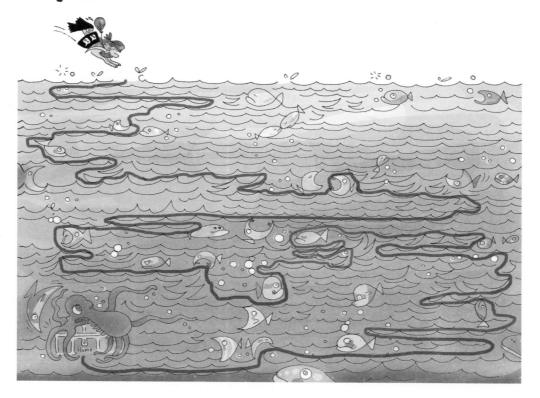

Uncle John's
FOR KIDS ONLY!

Monster Waves

So you want to be a sailor? You may change your mind after you read this.

What's a monster wave? One that rises 80 feet or more above the ocean's surface. Imagine a wall of water 1/4 mile wide and as high as a 10-story building bearing down on you like a freight train. That's a monster wave! Sometimes they're called "freaks" and "rogues." The biggest wave ever measured at sea was 98 feet tall. Most monster waves are caused by hurricanes and other storms. Others happen when waves join great ocean currents like the Gulf Stream. But wherever they come from, they're deadly—monster waves can snap a giant tanker ship in half like a toothpick. Worst of all, it takes hundreds of miles for one to build up to monster size. A ship can be sailing on a clear day far from a storm and still get slammed by a monster wave.

HARDY-HAR HAR-R-R!

Q: Why couldn't Captain Clueless learn the alphabet?

A: He was stuck at "c."

Pick a Lock

These ropes have been locked together. But they can all be separated by unlocking just one lock. Which one is it?

Answers
· · · · · · · · · · ·

Pick a Lock

Unlocking #2 will separate all the others.

The Creature from the Black Lagoon Has a No Good Very Bad Day

NOW IT'S YOUR TURN! Fill in the speech balloons on the comic page and then draw a second page to finish the story.

Uncle John's

FOR
KIDS
ONLY!

Answers

Pirate Pete's Log

Sea Animal Quiz

Bathing Beauty?

1. It's the only marine mammal that can live in fresh or salt water, as long as the water is shallow and warm.
2. Its closest relatives are elephants, hyraxes (a rabbit-sized rodent from the Middle East), and aardvarks.
3. It has three to four fingernails on each of its flippers.
4. It has a mouthful of wide, flat teeth called "marching molars." It constantly replaces them, just like a shark—when one falls out, another moves forward.
5. It has a tail shaped like a paddle.
6. It knows how to have fun in the water. It can do headstands, tail stands, somersaults, barrel rolls—even bodysurf!
7. It farts a lot! That's because it only eats plants—as much as 110 pounds a day.
8. It sounds like a mouse, with squeaks, whistles, and chirps.
9. A grown member of this species can be as big as a pickup truck.
10. When European sailors first saw this creature, they thought it was a mermaid.

WHAT IS IT?

RecoVERY

Number the pictures in order from dirtiest (1) to cleanest (8).

Extra Credit

The same string of three letters can complete each of these words:

B ________ ME
D ________ DE
R ________ RD
S ________ ND

Answers

· · · · · · · · · ·

Sea Animal Quiz

Answer: The Manatee

Let's face it—it's hard to imagine how ancient sailors could have mistaken the homely manatee for a beautiful mermaid, but they did. Commonly known as the sea cow, the manatee lives in the warm, shallow coastal waters of Florida, the Caribbean, Central America, Africa, and the Amazon. Its cousin, the dugong, lives in the South Pacific and Indian Oceans. Manatees are gentle, slow-moving animals with few natural enemies. In fact, humans are the cause of most manatee deaths. Some get sick from eating old fishing lines. Others get caught in "ghost nets"—nets that break off from fishing boats and drift through the ocean, trapping air-breathing mammals like dolphins, turtles, and manatees under water. But the worst manatee killer is the speedboat: It's a sad fact that researchers use scar patterns from propeller wounds to identify individual manatees.

Recovery

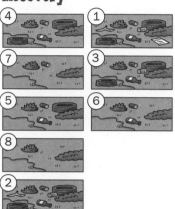

Extra Credit: ECO—become, decode, record, second